THE SPEED OF OUR LIVES

THE SPEED OF OUR LIVES

GRACE C. OCASIO

BLAZEVOX[BOOKS]
Buffalo, New York

THE SPEED OF OUR LIVES
by Grace C. Ocasio
Copyright © 2014

Published by BlazeVOX [books]

Printed in the United States of America

Interior design and typesetting by Geoffrey Gatza
Cover Art by Edwin Ocasio

First Edition
ISBN: 978-1-60964-171-9
Library of Congress Control Number: 2014930949

BlazeVOX [books]
131 Euclid Ave
Kenmore, NY 14217

Editor@blazevox.org

publisher of weird little books

BlazeVOX [books]

blazevox.org

21 20 19 18 17 16 15 14 13 12 01 02 03 04 05 06 07 08 09 10

BlazeVOX

for my father, Warner Walter Waters, Jr.

Acknowledgements

The poem "In Memory of Anne Frank" appeared in *Poetica: Reflections of Jewish Thought*; the poems "Homage to Audrey" and "To Lobengula, Great Warrior of Matabeleland" appeared in the magazine *Rapid River*; the poems "Hologram Dogwood" and "Savannah Blues–1946" appeared in the magazine, *Independence Boulevard*; the poems "Black Girl's Profile in 1948 of *Women of the Photo League Exhibit*," "To the City of Charlotte in the Year of Our Lord 1993: Wanted (Dead or Alive)," and "To a White Man Who Still Refuses to Recognize Huey Newton" appeared in the anthology, *Step Up to the Mic: A Poetic Explosion*; the poems "Father's Favorite Things and People" and "Inside" appeared in the literary journal *Transfer*; the literary journal *Rattle* published "Ars Poetica"; the online journal *The Cherry Blossom Review* published the poems "A Dare" and "The Cardinal"; the literary journal *The River's Edge* published "Arguing with Jesus" and "Notes on a Holland Stranger"; the Poetry Council of North Carolina published the poem previously titled "On Gershwin's Rhapsody in Blue" in its annual awards anthology, *Bay Leaves*; the poem "Reveries from Holden Beach" appeared in the chapbook, *Between the Lines: A Book of Words*; the poem "Odd April Day" appeared in the anthology *Meow Poetry: Fun, fabulous, feline verse*; the poem "Father's Sorrow" appeared in *Main Street Rag*; the literary journal *Drumvoices Revue* published "The Wright Origins," "Deposition," and "This Is the News"; the literary journal *Black Magnolias* published the poems "Emmett Till before His Eclipse" and "When I Consider"; the poems "Color like This," "Deeper than Skin," "Lost Boys of Sudan," "More than a Shoe," and "Walking Sepia" were published by the literary journal *Obsidian: Literature in the African Diaspora*; the poem "Requiem for Trees" was published by the Gwendolyn Brooks Writers Association of Florida, Inc. for their annual publication, *Revelry*; the poem "Sweet As Papayas" appeared in the literary journal *Earth's Daughters*; the poem "Light Sounds" appeared in *phati'tude Literary Magazine*; the poem "Strålande" appeared in *The Broad River Review*; the poems "Daedalus' View of Icarus' Fall" and "Trouble from the Start" were published by the online journal *Charlotte Viewpoint*; the poem "Purple Flush" was published by *Haight Ashbury Literary Journal*; the interdisciplinary e-journal *InTensions* published the poem "Matoaka, One Who Kindles (Also Known As Pocahontas)"; the electronic journal *Blast Furnace Press* published the poems "If I Get Married Again" and "Soul Man's Blues"; and the poem "Ruth, the Moabitess" was published by *Time of Singing*.

I'd like to thank my publisher, Geoffrey Gatza, for his unwavering support and enthusiasm in producing this book. I'd also like to thank the Carolina African American Writers' Collective for individual members' extensive feedback on many of the poems included in this collection. I also want to give credit to Jane Hirshfield for inspiring me to write the poem on Amy Winehouse.

Table of Contents

IV
Patriots 73

THE SPEED OF OUR LIVES

Introduction

Unpredictable Lives and Radiant Voices

Grace C. Ocasio's *The Speed of Our Lives* is a compelling collection of poems, which is grounded in history and a sense of place. She faithfully captures the spirits of these characters. The four sections of *The Speed of Our Lives* reveal glimpses into the lives of historical figures from American history from the 17th Century to the 20th Century. This volume of poetry speaks with clarity.

For example, here is the first stanza from the seventy-line poem, "Matoaka, One Who Kindles (Also Known As Pocahontas):"

> I have stood here many times at Werowocomoco,
> flicked my tongue in delight at the water.
> Above the water, my hands soared,
> moccasined feet danced on flat land,
> etched the figures of my father, Powhatan,

It is evident that Ocasio has read widely and transforms her insights into memorable poetry.

However, Ocasio is serious about her craft. Like the Harlem Renaissance writer Jessie Redmon Fauset's, Ocasio explores the extreme complexity of the characters she has chosen to include in her book. Yes, Ocasio takes on race, social issues and relationships without tiptoeing across the page. Like Rita Dove's poetry, *The Speed of Our Lives* explores subjects skillfully with attention to form, such as blues poems, kwansabas, minute poem, sestina, couplets and sequences. Like Sharon Olds' poetry, *The Speed of Our Lives* is daring and subtle at the same time. Like Gwendolyn Brooks' poetry, *The Speed of Our Lives* sings with grace and poignancy. Throughout this collection of poems, Grace C. Ocasio reports furiously.

So this is the book that will keep Ocasio's readers engaged. If one wants to know how a book can transcend unpredictable lives of characters and radiate voices, then step into *The Speed of Our Lives*, walk, read and listen. This is that kind of book: full of intellect and intensity.

Lenard D. Moore
Associate Professor of English
Mount Olive College
August 31, 2013

I
Sheroes

RUTH, THE MOABITESS

How does one imbibe
the breadth
of Ruth's act?
How she inched away
from her people,

Moabites,
genuflecting
in another direction
toward the ripe plains
of Bethlehem.

Ruth of people
who seared
their children.
Upon departing Moab,
she tilted her eye

toward Naomi.
And she slid
her hand
into Naomi's,
sized the length

and brevity
of her fingers.
What must have sprang
from her mouth?
A selah of a sigh

as she brushed
Naomi's fingertips,
glided
toward the palms
of her hands,

thumbed
their threadlike grooves.
As she cleaved
to Naomi,
she must have stalled,

receded one checked
moment,
revisited inhaling
charred flesh,
recalled how it blew

away before she realized
she should keep walking,
dust swirls shaping
with each step
she took.

QUEEN OF PERSIA: ESTHER

Were you a shy lisp
of a girl,
feet paddling
in Mordecai's direction,
your legs

a lopsided sprawl
as you waited
to see Hegai,
your way station
to King Xerxes?

I wish I knew more
than lore—
when your cousin
whisked
you away.

How old were you anyway?
Old enough to drive
into their dens
tears lurking
around your eyes?

Old enough to deflect disdain
in strangers' glances?
Old enough to tell fear
to go place itself
beside somebody else?

What did you ponder
when you stood–
a great gape
of a lass–
at Hegai's side?

What did you know
of perfumes?
Of lotions?
Of
silk?

I image you, rustling stalk of a girl
content to forage
in your cousin's groves.
There, lingering, safe
to loaf, roam, and stumble.

But King Xerxes' palace
must have daunted you,
brimming with scribes,
the gold and silver
glitter of couches.

Was it at his place you learned grace?
How to unruffle your hands,
unsheathe your smile,
stash your heart
in your golden chest?

Perhaps you knew that a heart
needs to be cordoned off,
stored in an ivory jewelry box
or a basket
lined with linen.

How could you know
kneeling and unkneeling
at the king's command
would propel you forward
to execute your cousin's plan?

How many times did you dip
your hands in cream?
Turn your head
at Hegai's cue?
Powder purplish blue your eyelids?

You must have twisted,
whirled on your errand
to inform Xerxes
of Haman's plot to discard,
like shriveled scrolls, all Jews.

When you neared Xerxes,
did your toes cramp?
Did your heart lurch
like trees on a windy day?
Did your words catch like a glitch?

Then to witness how his staff
did not falter
must have made you
swing your arms,
giddy as a shepherd boy.

Xerxes
must have eyed you,
noticed how
your skin gleamed
like his marble pillars.

He must have trusted,
woman
that you were,
spying deep in your eyes,
your people's sackcloths,

rent into thousands
of pieces
the bloody strips
revolving in the vortices
of your eyes.

Note

Haman the Agagite drafted a decree calling for the annihilation of the Jewish people
dwelling in provinces King Xerxes had dominion over.

MATOAKA, ONE WHO KINDLES (ALSO KNOWN AS POCAHONTAS)

I have stood here many times at Werowocomoco,
flicked my tongue in delight at the water.
Above the water, my hands soared,
moccasined feet danced on flat land,
etched the figures of my father, Powhatan,

and my brothers. I swing my tattooed arms, arch
them at the sky. My neck glistens with white beads.
Listen, now, as I wail a tune. Witness how I bend
into wind, consider how my fists stir
this great river. The mighty Powhatan has fallen.

He rolls and tumbles, tumbles and rolls
in his deep, death walk. He rises now before me,
pumps his arms as though rowing
a boat, shakes worse than a doe.
His teeth stab his tongue. And I turn away

ashamed to embrace what his actions tell me.
When I turn back to him, he is gone.
I raise my arms and press my palms
against the sky. Do you hear me? I, a woman
warrior for my people, slap treaties

from your hands. I hurl beans in your eyes,
those of you who sought to barter
away my people. I, who am Matoaka, ask
you why you sacked my father's village.
Wasn't it enough that I draped my skin

in your petticoats, bodice, and lace,
paraded myself before your king
and your poet, Ben Jonson, who gawked
at the hue of my flesh? How I wish
I had taunted you, disemboweled your vowels,

skinned your consonants, cast your words
away, syllable by putrid syllable, shoved them
into firewood, stirred them until they
exploded into flame. I remember
John Smith's eyes, how they drifted over me.

He didn't know I mocked
his loose gaze. I'd pretend
his eyes were targets my arrows' points
would pierce and shatter into tiny shards.
And what of my husband, John Rolfe?

When I first met him, my eyes ran,
prowled around his head, his shoulders,
his feet, until they were satisfied.
Although my heart did not guffaw
with glee, it did not lie down, either.

I decided then I could stride to his love,
prop his love on all sides of me
like pillows. Now I shift in the wind,
shake out my bird-nest thick black hair,
heavy as hemp, that swings to my knees.

I wrap my mantle about me, sing
of werowances who strung bows
at my father's command, sprang over gullies,
scoured the woods for uttasantasough.
Into this bay, I nestle myself and breathe

in my ancestors' sighs, groans,
and screeches. My left palm plants itself
on the ground and listens for whispers
of my mother's and my grandmother's
and my great-grandmother's and my great-

great-grandmother's words and hears them all—
a waterfall of sound rising into the crevices
of my body. I tingle from scalp
to toe. As my ancestors' words gush
through me, I am what you did not know,

what you did not wish to know, this tapping
on a tree trunk, the patter of feet trampling leaves.
If you do not hear me, you will dream
of yourself drowning, become as untethered
as a pebble among many grains of sand.

<u>Notes</u>

1) Werowocomoco-Powhatan's village
2) Powhatan-paramount chief of local Algonkian-speaking tribes during the time of Jamestown settlement
3) Werowance-chief
4) Uttasantasough-Algonkian word for English

STRÅLANDE
(*for Garbo*)

The photographer who traced you,
month after month,
chafed when your fingers

subtracted your face.
The words you once intoned,
I want to be alone,

coursed like waves in his eardrums.
Strålande, those shimmering words
that slid off your tongue,

arpeggio of notes
sprinting across strings.
The unmistakable depth of your face—

chiseled stone that didn't blanch
or flinch
at the camera's glint,

angular in its arrangement.
You could wear
any clothes—

trousers, couture gowns, clogs.
Hands, lithe as a mime's.
Your voice—base cello.

Critics mocked you.
One cartoonist penciled
you into caricature—

you, a figure mouthing
one word—*Ouch!*
as a campfire blaze

spread beneath your foot.
Your foot dangled,
barely grazed by flames.

An assortment of men
loathed the lilt of your vowels,
shunned the tilt of your face.

What you left the world
is a room steeped in your rhythm,
a voice when heard

little girls choose rumbas
over pirouettes.
Thanks to the wide arc of your gaze,

your movies arrest.
Like a prime perfume,
you settle into our skin.

<u>Note</u>

Strålande means "glorious" or "brilliant" in the Swedish language.

IN MEMORY OF ANNE FRANK

Anne, I see your face before me,
your eyes kindled like a kerosene lamp.

Did they, the German soldiers, taunt you?
Did they tell you your hair wasn't pretty enough,
that your hair resembled an opossum's?

Their words still hang on your hideout's walls,
putrid and slimy.

You could never tear them down.
You wielded this aspect of stilled lips—
not a smile, nor a frown.

In the only picture I've ever scanned of you,
your hair gleams like a phonograph record.

I unlock that expression on your face,
carry it in my hands
like a corsage or diamond pin.

I tilt your visage sideways,
at an angle,
even flip it upside down,
marvel at the vastness of your countenance,
vaulting over the demure and puny decades
that stagger under its weight.

Then I replace that cast.
Place it back on your face.

Anne, please tell me how you are now.
Do you roam through meadows?
Do you stroll through gardens swelling with African marigold
and black jack gladiolus?

Is the look
on the cover of your diary
still with you?

Or has that image been recalled,
squirreled away by God's own hands,
never to remind you
of your earthly life's specks
and sputters?

I envision you now,
all the kinks in your life
rooted out of your smile.

HOMAGE TO AUDREY
(for Audrey Hepburn)

You were a silk sleeve of a girl at thirteen
When you disarmed a blunt German soldier's face—
One who had come through the trees.

You saluted him with wild flowers and a smile.
He dismissed you with a pat on your shoulder.
And you went skipping away.

What would he have done
Had he known just seconds before his arrival
You had conspired with his enemy—a British paratrooper?

At fourteen you, poised
With two twig arms
That fanned out

Toward your third-world future
To wrap around oblong bodies
With too narrow faces.

Near Arnhem in 1945,
All it took was seven bars of chocolate
From Allies to rouse you out of your World War II stupor.

In 1954, you sat,
Pensive finger crooked in mouth,
Eyes reeling in your Oscar from the stage.

Sure, you were human, but you didn't complain.
All you ever said during your UNICEF stint
Was *I get very tired.*

HOLOGRAM DOGWOOD

Suddenly I notice the Angela Davis of 1970
in dogwood leaves,
hair billowed on her head,

her hair, more lavish
than a Carmen Miranda headpiece,
her hair, a dark mass,

towering over her luminous face
that could appear so stern and solemn
in newspaper photos.

Angela was the REVOLUTION,
her bright fist
saluting the sky,

in black turtle neck
and black pants, she stood,
the Eiffel Tower.

WALKING SEPIA
(for Michelle Obama)

Draped in your lime green dress, Michelle.
Your grin stalled clouds.
Your stride scrubbed air.
The wide expanse

Of your Moor brown skin millions scanned—
Wheelchair-bound men,
Girls with spiked bangs,
Women in furs.

You swirled in a one-strap white gown.
Arms whisked away
Flash bulbs and gasps,
Yells and whispers.

PURPLE FLUSH
(*for Janis Joplin*)

Your song "Maybe" gusts into my ears.
I scramble to turn its volume down,
but your voice clings to the lyrics,
wills me to keep your sound loud.

On my way back from D.C.,
I blare your "Bye, Bye Baby"
into my car.
I drive into rain as your shriek

warns me I'd better stop for the red light.
What kind of blues would you mesh
with today's rock n' roll, rhythm n' blues,
or folk music? I never meddle with the dial

when your voice coaxes air to heed
your commands. I wonder, with a voice
like that, how'd you end up alone in a room
with a dubious kilo of heroin?

How'd your body sway from bed to floor?
My eyes stalk these pages for intimations
of who you were. I glean you
dressed up your hair with boa feathers,

sometimes ensconced yourself in fur.
Those feathers—replete in green, red,
purple hues—crowned your head,
framed your auburn strands.

The granny glasses I spy
on your greatest hits album cover
startle me.
I wish I'd been there to yank the tequila

out of your hand, diminish the purple flush
of overdose from your cheeks.
Why'd you insist on deveining yourself?
Your notes that straddle air

clamp down on my shoulders,
urge me to claw apart each second of the day,
slash words that sputter on the page,
wrench from my wrists and hips rhythm.

You in purple, welded-to-thigh
pants. You, utterer of oracles on stage
with your Big Brother band. You, pressing
a tambourine into your flesh.

Your voice erases the droopiness
in my steps, silences
the stutter of windshield wipers,
blather of car horns, staccato of rain.

CARDS

The headline "Amy Winehouse dead" blares as travelers drift by.
Did death come to her in fine lace, showering her with applause?
Did Britney, Beyoncé, and Lady Gaga shuffle the news,
put down her cards
as if just holding them
would burn their hands?

ALONDRA DE LA PARRA

Anhinga, she sways like sweet grass,
twirls the baton wand in her hand.

Her torso undulates, arms weave into air
Mozart's *The Marriage of Figaro*.

One minute her fingers simulate *Swan Lake*.
The next minute her feet split into rumba.

The music streams from her fingers,
swirls through the wand she sprinkles

the violinists and violists with until their notes crest
into a stratosphere of glissandos. Pine trees

behind the stage can't resist her wrist's promptings,
hula as her arms climb over music stands.

Maestra de la batuta, *Muy bien.*
Los queremos mucho, she says, bowing.

The sheen of her black pants illuminates the stage
as she exits to a glaze of afternoon sunlight.

Note

Alondra de la Parra is a Mexican conductor. She is the first Mexican woman to conduct
a concert in New York City.

II
She Revolutionary

ON THE OTHER SIDE

The night after Harlem didn't sleep
when Joe Louis stopped Max Schmeling
in the first round, a girl sat on the side of a street
where a bridge and ladder lay.
She longed to streak across the ocean
that stretched out before her on the other side
of the street. Stale from life, she was crusty
as Italian bread left out over night on a stoop.

Still, she marveled at birds.
She wanted to kiss a wren.
One day she saw one land in a maze of tree limbs.
She whispered to it, crossed,
uncrossed her arms to lure him.
He tilted his head, cast a bleary eye in her direction
Razor blade straight, she tossed her head,
pirouetted three times, and time stepped on oak leaves.

Then this bird did an odd thing:
flew into her hand, nudged his beak against her palm.
The girl beamed until she looked up at the sky,
witnessed how a plane grazed it.
Suddenly, the sky turned black and she keened.
Her little wren noticed her littered face,
glided out of her hand,
until its back rested against sky.
He flew backward, then forward,
until the sky sparkled like nail polish.
He flew back into the girl's hand,
found her staring at the ocean.

She did a strange thing: she yodeled.
Her voice bounced up and down on her side
of the street, rippled the ocean.
The wren circled above her head.
The girl thumped her chest,
pressed her face against the ground.
When she raised her head,
she shook her hair, then pulled it out.
Her wren gathered her hair, rearranged it like a nest.
She put it back on her head, patted it down,

splayed her arms, reaching for the other side.

The girl whirled toward the bridge,
which lay on its side
a few feet away from her.
She stared at the bridge. Her bird chirped five times.
She held in her breath and blew
until the bridge towered above her,
spanned the ocean.
The girl glowed, clapped her hands, gamboled.
Out of the corner of her eye, she spotted the ladder.
She spun around, raced to the ladder, yanked
it upward, pushed it against the bridge.
She scrambled up the ladder with one hand
until her feet connected with the bridge.

She padded a few steps forward and stopped.
What does the water look like? she wondered.
She leaned over the railing
of the right side of the bridge,
eyed the water moving topsy-turvy.
She could not go on.
Her toes curled like snakes. Limp as worms,
her arms hung from her sides.
She saw numbers marching in front of her.
She stuttered, walked in circles.
The wren pecked the top her head, made her blink.

On the other side, she was a breath, sigh, and shout.
Shoeless, she watched rain pound puddles
between her toes.
A grin flared on her face.
Her wren nestled into her shoulder.
Against a black bridge,
she, a shimmer,
head to toe.

BLACK GIRL'S PROFILE IN 1948 OF *WOMEN OF THE PHOTO LEAGUE EXHIBIT*

The black girl in this picture is pre-sixties.
She is pre-revolution.
See the lack of revolution

In her hair—how it fits snug as a skullcap
Against her head.
Yet her skin is revolutionary.

Yes, it's exotic.
All that black glistening
Against a white backdrop.

And as for her features,
Her lips are two perfectly shaped slopes,
Her neck slightly protruding

Like a microphone in its stand.
As I study her,
I am stunned by her face—

How it opens up to the camera.
How, shimmering in its blackness,
It obscures the glare of white around it.

TO THE CITY OF CHARLOTTE IN THE YEAR OF OUR LORD
1993: WANTED (DEAD OR ALIVE)

I thought you were the New South.

Piping-hot-ready, I steamed
For you in June that year
When smoke rose
And the air squawked
From David Koresh's threat.

I thought a lush city,
Brimming with cherry blossoms,
Azaleas and dogwoods,
Would welcome, waving me in
Like a traffic cop.

But I was wrong.

What I received
Was a lack of grace:
Glances some unsteady
As china clattering to the floor.

What I wanted was a nod—
A surveyor,
Appraising my skin,
Finding it of more value
Than a million
Treasury notes.

Brazen in look,
You tore through me
With a razor-blade thin gaze,
Prized open every ounce
As if I were a prisoner on death row

Bound to confess why my skin is yellow,
Why I am wed to another
Sort of like me but not quite,
His skin like banana flesh.

I am a native daughter.
Stories of my ancestors,
Those from Sylvania, Georgia,
And Charleston County
Roil through my bloodstream.

I am not a fiction,
Pickaninny on plantation
Strumming banjo
Singing with twang,
Strutting my way

Through Mr. Jefferson's Monticello
Where slave spirits surround me,
Sway arms like tall grass,
Chant a mulatto blues song
In the wheat fields.

Beside my husband,
I have faced
The bleary-eyed mantra
Of your grimace and ordered you off
My body's premises.

ARS POETICA

They laughed when I asked
for pancetta,
those grocery store clerks.

I don't care.
It's better to be chic
than to lie

in some bland corner
of a room,
wilting and frumpy.

What do I care
about the woman
who never dares to don

a houndstooth jacket?
It's up to us to set
the speed of our lives.

Audrey, for instance,
could dazzle
simply by placing

an ordinary swatch
against her skin:
chiffon, silk, organza.

To the nay-sayers I say
if you choose to live
like toads, why should I care?

It would have been easier
to ask for Italian bacon.
But isn't it better

to be swift than rushed?
Better to be svelte than thin?
Better to seek than to settle?

SWEET AS PAPAYAS

I pushed. You fell,
legs unraveling like chains of a swing.
You damned me to dwell in a tent of longing.
I violated our contract, aborted it,

creating a breach that can never be erased
unless one of us
is brave enough to unwind it.

How will I convince God some day
I was right to seal you off,
as if you were a canyon-wide hole
in a blanched wall of my brain?

Mom, on this planet, seconds and minutes
can taste sweet as papayas
if we let them.

We are fools, living in this squalor of silence,
treating each other
like white collar criminals.

I want to take you in my arms and say,
There is an end to this.
The end—me, blotting out our mottled past,

beseeching you to pardon,
you, lush in your plump skin,
breathing my face.

LIGHT SOUNDS

I have always loved rhythm,
listening to Billie Holiday blare blues
into my ears and heart,

to hear the hum of violins and trumpets,
harmonicas and harpsichords.
I have always loved the sound

of rain strumming its own tune
on the roof of a house,
loved the silky sound

of pitter-pattering feet on carpet,
loved the echo at Carnegie Hall,
sounds so lush they flush out the vile.

I have always loved the oboe
and how its lilting sound resonates
in the air,

loved the scratchy sound
of a needle on a phonograph record,
loved the sound

of my father scatting to himself
in his jazzy tones.
I have always loved the rhythm

of his head shaking to the sound
of Coltrane or Gillespie.
I have always heard his tenor

over and over in my head
like water trickling down
onto a countertop.

I have always loved the sound
of my hands feeling
the grooves of a phonograph record,

loved the sound of love
in kisses and hugs and handshakes,
starts and nods and solemn stares.

A DARE

I sing of my limbs,
twirl like a four-year-old ballerina.

I am the one who startles the dawn,
unhinges the night,
dishevels the wind's breath.

And I am a whistle, branch, and shiver.

The girl unlocking myself,
I dare you to fly into my arms.

Shadow me
as if your life depends on it.

NOTES ON A HOLLAND STRANGER

He sat smug in a striped shirt,
His lunch on a small, round table.
I noticed the static in his heart.

When he waved, did he wonder
If I'd fix it?
I barely looked his way again.

Yet I stashed his image in my sleeve anyway.
As I walked out the door, the back of my head detected
How his eyes stole across my buttocks and legs.

I was aghast that he could mimeograph my body so clearly.
When I got into my car,
He hailed me with directions to the bookstore

I had overlooked on a street as unknown to me as Sanskrit.
When he leaned near me,
His breath sounded all around me: on the steering wheel,

On the dashboard, in the glove compartment of my car.
Finally it settled itself on my wedding band.
Is that significant? he asked, grinning.

I paused and murmured, *yes.*
Then this look scrawled itself like a child's first letters
Across his face, and I was sad.

Sad I had to roll up my window and say good-bye.
Sad my hands couldn't erase the longing on his face.

IF I GET MARRIED AGAIN

I promise I'll wear shimmering gold lipstick,
dance a thousand jigs before dusk.

All my bells will flap their tongues when I
unscroll my life like a map for my love.

There'll be no blues to stoke the fire.
No more will I hear those Bessie Smith moans.

The bridesmaids' hair will blow like Spanish moss,
their hair ribbons fly like cranes.

Mist will airbrush night
followed by daybreak's auburn glint.

I'll sing, wave my glass, whirl across my lawn.
The clink of crystal around me will slit air.

I'll hear the chime of my clock,
catch a flight to Spain.

III

Princes and Privates

DAEDALUS' VIEW OF ICARUS' FALL

When I saw Icarus barreling down,
I knew I should have
placed my own body in his way.

Instead, I watched him,
his arms flailing,
a high-pitched shriek.

How I wished
he had been bored with his wings,
weary of cumulus clouds,

cruising over the sea, musing
simple pleasantries of Sicily—
an amber garden, copious dune.

What if I had devised a contraption
that called for him
to be strapped to me?

If only I had designed
sun-proof, glove-like wings
that caught heat, hurled it back.

Now all I do
is contemplate greeting the king
of Sicily, sonless.

How to tell the king about my loss?
I will regale him
with a story

about a boy who wandered
until his feet blistered,
forced to suspend his journey.

ARGUING WITH JESUS

There are times in this vast room
when I have courage to stand up to Him.
I say: *No. No more. None of this.*
It will have to go.
As if I could rake up all my pain
into one big pile to be burned.

He says: *It's a gift.*

Then He gathers up all my pain and pushes it
toward me in a barrel,
until He stops it in front of me.

And I say: *Thank you.*
I will wrap it around me like a cloak.

He says: *Good, child. Never take it off.*

I say: *Yes, never. The girl or boy,*
man or woman who attempts to tear it
from me will have to strip my skin.

TO LOBENGULA, GREAT WARRIOR
OF MATABELELAND

White dogs, you screamed,
when you discovered
that Rhodes and his loons
bilked you out of your land.

But you had trusted
in the white man's magic—
those starch-collared crisp lips
of imperialism that could blend

words until they sounded sweet
as the trill of the coqui.
You trusted those Britishers
to treat you right

and not deplete the land.
You were one monolith of a man.
Your tribesmen called you
"The Great Elephant."

Your breast bulged with a keen,
glittery heart, too bright for those white dogs.
You see, they couldn't withstand
your light.

That's why they plied you
with morphine.
They wanted to make your heart's
light falter.

But just when they thought
they had quashed it,
you dimmed down your light yourself,
left them flailing in darkness.

LOST BOYS OF SUDAN

I

After I read about you in *Life*,
I pictured your frown,
your shoulders hunched
as you squatted,
chewed for survival.

No equation could balance
your fate.

Back when you foraged
in the bush
you depleted
your strength,
rested hands
against your spent faces.

Now,
what lingers?

Some teetering memories
of a lion's breath?

II

In a new world—
refugees—
you will master the mundane:
washing and drying clothes,
scrubbing pots and pans,
crossing streets.

Long ago,
you waxed braver than pharaohs.

I wish I could
slap time's face
for making you wait
to sift through
this new world.

These days each of you
draws handshakes, hugs.

My hands brush
the black and white
print of your faces.

III

What was it like
to defy
the lion's logic?

What was it like
to feel your bodies
falter
from the pressure
of each mile
rolling away
beneath your feet?

To dodge the sun
shamassa, to flee
from his heavy hand?

You trampled odds
that would have thinned
the average person's blood
to broth.

That old Khartoum,
city of perennial weeping
where sin greeted you
in the guise of glue.

Your senses
whirled into mist
that enveloped you.

I who jangle in my skin implore you
to spread your dreams in America
like a Japanese silk fan,
stack nights like facts,
gather years like reeds.

<u>Note</u>

In a *Life* magazine article, issue date June 1, 1988, author Katherine Seligman chronicled the harrowing experiences of a group of boys called the "Lost Boys." In an effort to find relief from the deplorable conditions they faced, the lost boys often sniffed glue, their way of getting "high." The term "shamassa" means "the children who run under the sun." Writer Edward Barnes detailed further the boys' plight in a *Life* article that appeared in the magazine's June 1992 issue. Years later, *The Charlotte Observer* published an article (December 22, 2001) in which the journalist, Diane Suchetka, noted how a small number of the lost boys had migrated to America, residing in certain cities of the Southeast.

ON *RHAPSODY IN BLUE*

Each time I hear the siren call of the clarinet,
I forget the boy in eighth grade
who jinxed me with a slap.
Suddenly I see him, Gershwin,
wand thin in his tux, bowing,
his nimble legs stretching as he sits
on the piano bench.
One foot reaches the pedal
while the other taps,
keeping time with the rhythm
in his head.
And what happens next
is a mystery.
Fingers sprawl across black and white keys,
thump out a melody
that unhinges the audience.
Carnegie Hall is a maze
of lights. I listen, listen—to an allegro
of notes skidding
across the keyboard.
Faces whirr
by as the piano roll holds sway.
Clara Bow, Joan Crawford,
Norma Shearer, Garbo—
flap, furious as bats
to the trills.
Whenever I imagine the sheen
of a Boston train shifting
in the wind,
I also conjure Gershwin
charting notes with his pen.
And when the great cymbals clash,
I become the woman
who can't say no
to dancing barefoot across a bridge.
But then Gershwin slows everything
down again—
decrescendo in my veins.

SOUL MAN'S BLUES
(*for James Brown*)

He could shake his way around the edge of
a dime and never lose the smile on his face.

— Marc Eliot

I came out dead as can be.
Glad Aunt Minnie whacked me 'til I could see.
Said I came out dead as can be.
Minnie whacked me 'til I could see.

In those early years,
home was just a shack.
No plumbing, no electricity.
Not even flour to make a flapjack.

Learned to glide on my feet.
Spiffed up wingtips,
snatched wallets,
picked cotton for meat.

One day Mama and Papa split.
Papa stepped in and out
of my world.
So I had me a fit.

At fifteen, I jimmied cars,
went to jail at sixteen.
Holed up, I moaned
'bout sleepin' behind bars.

Bobby Byrd helped me break jail.
Set free, took to baseball
'til my leg let me down.
Felt like a porch with no rail.

My tongue tried gospel,
switched to rhythm n' blues.
With "Please, Please, Please,"
I snagged ladies from pews.

Over the years,
a car overturned my boy Teddy's life.
Hits slowed down.
I battled my fourth wife.

Still I kept croonin',
swoll up in 1986
with "Living in America."
That song's my baddest mix.

Gone now that shack of early days.
I cling to the soil.
Gone now that shack of early days.
I cling to the soil.
No shack here: I'm restin',
shrouded in afternoon haze.

JOHN F. KENNEDY, JR.
(*for John-John*)

Take, for instance,
the photo
of you
kneeling
on one leg—
your body braced
for assistance
as you peer
in the direction
of the little
black boy
whose body
angles
toward your own
the lone hand his
barely grazes
your scarf.
One might consider
the way you
answered questions
pausing
with a breath
or two
words
scattered
here and there
no more,
no less.
Something
in the way
you set
your hands
proffered them
before that sleek
crowd
at the Democratic
Convention of '88,
how you stood
flyweight-like
on your feet.

So much so
it seems
a strong wind
might have made
your body
dance
one full
minute
before you could
regain
composure.
No,
I do not
relegate you
to the status
of frigid cold
myth to square
shoulders with Adonis.
Instead, I'll tell you
what I saw
in you.
Simple as this:
you were
the distant cousin
I'd inquire about
from time to time.
I cheered you
each instance
you rebuffed
flashes
of light
sent your way
by photographers
keen
on exalting your
image.
Yes,
you were
precise.
You navigated
your way
through
the front door
of a New York City

transit bus.
The intricacy
of your position
short circuits my brain.
When
I study you,
I perceive no
mirror, no mirage.
I picture you
hunkered down
in stands
at Yankee Stadium
with pretzel
in hand
and glancing
over your shoulder
at a friend
or tapping fingers
on desk.
No,
I did not
know you.
But what I like
best
about you
is how well
you could scramble
to your feet,
look into
the distance
shrug your shoulders
mumble under
your breath
to some onlooker
Pretty day, isn't it?
and saunter off
into a frenzy
of shuttle flights
and galas.

SOUNDS FULL OF HOLES: AT THE GROUP HOME FOR
SPECIAL NEEDS ADULTS (*for WWW, III*)

I knew you before you knew me,
my kin. I adore your vowels.
I salute your howls.

You, clunky in your clothes.
Remember the time you jerked
away from me,
how I grabbed you?
how I clenched air?
how we slid into the street?

You nearly struck me down,
the force of you greater than
a pick-up truck
on an icy road.

No skid marks on my skin,
just raw hands from our struggle.

Now, tight as a folded chair,
you squirm on the sofa, grunt.
I scroll through you,
swallow my thoughts,
watch you slumber. I say,
I was the one in the crumpled up picture.

Eeeeeeeeeeeeee, you say to me.
I take my paring knife to your vowels,
chop them up, grind them thinner
than pulled veal.
Ask you to recite your sounds:
repeat, repeat, repeat.

I poke a hole in your shrieks,
click the switch for mute—
silence us.

We sway, stumble
through our past.
I clutch your wrist.

You at ten. I at five.
I say, *No, I never blow bubbles
when I chew gum.*

You big brother
to middle brother and me.
No, I don't play with Cracker Jacks.

Yes, go ahead and tickle my toes.
Yes, I do scribble all over myself.
We tousle each other's hair,

track each other's giggles.
In my adult flesh, I stack my words,
place them on the dinner table.

Your breath devours them.
Eeeeee-iiiiii, you say?
I thumb the fine print of your hands.

THE CARDINAL

Outside my kitchen window,
This cardinal illumined my bush.
On each other we spied, general to soldier,
Eye to eye, nose to beak.

At first, I loathed him.
The bright hot pepper redness of his breast
Dulled my circuit board vision.
It took three blinks to recover my sight.

The brewing quarrel of his black eye
Spilled over, dousing me with its hot words.
Yet I could not ease myself away from him.
Just before I was about to woo him,

Unleashing my soprano to fall like a downpour
On his ears, he flitted away.
I was left wondering in which direction
His wings edged the horizon.

REVERIES FROM HOLDEN BEACH

Far away a city
croons to me,
a sidewalk glistens in its skin.

Far away from the whirr of waves
a name slides from the lips
of a man in a tiny kitchen.

He rouses two boys—dogs,
huddles with them,
preps them how to vault

over my absence:
a pause of two days.
He sways, drops his head,

whispers a prayer,
as his shoes strike twigs.
On the patio

his tongue completes its trill
as I lean into the sun,
spread my arms across dunes,

then scat about a place solid
beneath my feet
as this wooden step.

REQUIEM FOR TREES

Toppled trees
in my front yard,
I do not know
how to miss them.

Intrusive
as Greek gods,
they baffle humans
who tower over them.

Who were they?
One poplar, two red oaks,
two hickories the wind now
salutes through cackles.

I whistle, dismiss
bag pipes, fife.
Shuffle, slide, shimmy,
flex my wrists,

scan them for squirrels'
teeth marks,
crows' dung,
praying mantis wings.

My fingers flirt,
skate across bark
coarse as barbed wire.
I gloat that they've

been zapped.
Unruly trees
once concealed
brick and bow window.

TROUBLE FROM THE START

First, you pawed down the utility room blinds.
Then, your fear of pulsing light shadowed you:
each time it leapt onto the ceiling
your brain tumbled into its ditch,
your bark so foul I'd stash
you in the half bath to quell you.

Greedy, too,
you'd land in Blondie's and Spunky's food
even before you'd consider your own,

but you could also do
what you were supposed to:
lick Papa Eddie's feet, nap by the fireplace, howl
when hearing sirens.

I sometimes tested, upended you as I edged
into the bathroom. You didn't even wince.

But when you lunged at me
like a sumo wrestler, my heart stalled.
Last thing I eyed was your yellow teeth
sinking into my wrist.

Hours later, all I saw were traces
of your beige and rust fur
underneath the bathroom door.

ODD APRIL DAY

I, giddy with the scent of haiku
in the air. The crunch of road
taunted my foot, dared me

to bear down harder on the pedal.
Dust clutched the road.
My eyes tracked a white flash—

a flag, a kite, a scarf—in the road.
A sound like a screen door
banging shut shook my ears.

My car slowed to a drone.
I didn't want to drive back
to the spot, but my conscience

spun me 'round. My foot released
itself on the pedal, and I coasted
toward her. She greeted me,

lifted her specked paw as though
ready to mew like a chanteuse
and then shuddered one long spell

of a second. Drenched in blood,
her chin, red as a scarlet poppy.
My eyes refused to abandon her.

Last time I saw her,
she lay, chin nestled
into the road that became her blanket.

IV
Patriots

SAVANNAH BLUES—1946
(*for WWW, Jr.*)

It's a soft voice of a grandma whispering to her Negro
Grandchild, the timbre of her voice like a cracked whistle:
"Chile, chile, you know it ain't fair being black,
As blue as you can be
It's just the way it be,
The way it be."

It's a blue-black clatter that explodes in somebody's commode,
As a black boy rants above the toilet's drone:
"My papa done told me I ain't worth nothin'.
He the one that say I took Mama away.
He say I'm lurchin' like a street urchin
Each and every day."

It's a little colored boy scuttling down a half-and-half street,
Avoiding the white glares that speak
From corners of bland windows:
"That there boy is lazy.
All day long he shambles 'round.
That there boy is crazy.
All day long he stomps through town."

It's a grandma raspin' as she carries her grandson on her back:
"Chile, chile, I'm just as blue as you.
Your grandpa, he goes 'bout his bizness,
Just like I'm some old shoe.
I done told you once if I done told you twice
This being colored jazz is a thankless thang."

It's a brown boy, shufflin' through photos
Of almost white uncles,
Gropin' for his grandpa's sesame seed skin mutterin',
"I'm so sorry, Papa, that I'm a bit darker than the others.
Darker than all the rest."

FATHER'S SORROW

I will never forget
My father's shimmering Vodka lips
Blurting, *Bluesette, don't you fret.*

He was nothing
But a sway and swoon
In his armchair.

I wanted to wring his soggy brain dry.
Let his head rest on my arm
Like a hammock.

And I would sing to him,
Smooth as Sarah Vaughan,
Scratchy as Billie Holiday,

No, Daddy, no.
Don't fret.
'Bluesette' ain't nothing but a song.

PAPA'S PATE

Mama takes my place on my bed—the sofa.
I just want to sleep in my bed.
I long to tumble into my dreams.
Papa stands—his face shifts into a scowl.
I totter until my feet land on the stairs.
Papa shouts around the corner, shaking his pate.

I gawk, humbled by the golden pate
that butted me off the sofa,
spun me in the way of the staircase.
I cough, slump against this upstairs bed
and grimace, remembering Papa scowling.
Nothing is as tall as my dreams.

Papa hovers over my dreams.
His visage I see, huge as the moon's pate.
I used to wonder why he'd scowl
as he lounged, drunk on the sofa.
Now I scurry to a boardless bed,
flee from shadows' stares.

Backwards, I climb the steps,
galumph to my dreams
that lie collapsed on the berth.
My fists rap a tune on Papa's pate.
Mama's snoring rattles, hurts my ears—so far
away, his face, devoid of its scowl.

From step to step, I recoil from a scowl of a mask,
curse the hands that built these stairs,
stupid in their weight, stealing me from the sofa.
I scuttle to my dreams
that will blot out Papa's patina,
sink into my lopsided bed.

Moonlight pours onto my bunk,
turns Papa's glare into a ghost scowl
that rises and towers over my organ lamp's pate.
I shrug off sheets, shamble to the stairs,
stumble in the hallway where I conjure dreams
more lush than a quilt-covered sofa.

Now I eye this pate that chased me to the stairs,
overturn my bed, rebuff the scowl,
lurch in my dreams, rise to a mangled sofa.

MORE THAN A SHOE

I

I conjure you now,
swifter than the sorceress raised Samuel.

Summon you to my office room,
ask what happened to your words?

When I sat next to you, I tried
to draw you closer than a handle to its blade.

I tried to hold your gaze,
though your eyes always found a way to stray.

Now what I see is you shaking your head,
no answer.

The slight movement of your head tells me
I better put down my words.

Brandishing them at you, I carry
high-powered rifles.

It's your sudden glance that leaves me
stuttering.

II

I am alone now.
Alone, I said.

I am counting like a stopwatch,
counting past thoughts you kept to yourself,

Counting past the day you slapped me for wanting sleep
when there wasn't even a bed.

I am counting past the day of your death:
the fifth, eighth, nineteenth, thirtieth,

Counting moments between us like lights
flickering seconds before a power outage,

Counting gray hairs on your head,
your love cached in small gestures,

Lugging suitcases to the freshman room door,
a Howard sticker placed on your rear window.

Yes, I remember your love doled
out to me as money.

But Dad, we never hugged,
not in parting even.

Only the wave of your hand,
a slight nod of your head.

In the distance, I detected you
as I settled into my seat.

III

So now, when I see you I stare.
You are this beautiful urn that lies in this niche.

In your porcelain body you stand.
Stems of blue flowers adorn you.

Sentinel-like,
you guard the glass encasing you.

Standing opposite you,
I read your gold-plated dates: 1936 to 1987.

My tears blur you.
I wonder why God graphed only five decades for you.

IV

It was Mom who called the day you died.
She said she watched the cardiograph halt.

Dad, I screamed.
Dad, I just wanted to help you.

I don't remember hanging up the phone.
It was a pay phone I sprinted to.

I let the cord dangle after I screamed.
And every man I passed on the street looked like you.

I can still picture you waving.
No, it is not you.

It is me dangling by the phone.
Somehow I got back to my room.

Mom must have heard the static in my voice.
An ambulance arrived.

Mom said the paramedics were there.
You refused to go at first, she said.

In my room at the YWCA,
day faded, I was alone.

Night poured in.
Shadows from car lights dashed across the walls.

V

Pop, man thin as a shoe,
I learn to live outside your skin.

INSIDE

You stared out
through the cracks
of the window.

Eyes broadening.
Hands twitching.
You paced the floor

for one minute.
Then two minutes.
Then five minutes more.

You kneeled on the floor
with your toes
touching the carpet.

You got up from the floor,
picked up a glass,
hurled it against a wall.

You yelled out *God*
before you punched yourself
in the chest.

You started laughing.
Your arms shook,
Your nostrils spread.

Then you spit on the carpet.
You crossed yourself
before you went down.

COLOR LIKE THIS

Pop never wore brown pants.
But I knew black men who did.

Growing up, I spied them
in brown slacks and shirts

at barbershops, lounges, chicken
and rib joints, pool halls.

Why'd they wear that color?
Didn't they know brown sours?

I knew brown as the furrows
above Pop's brows.

The rust-colored water to drink,
pop's stomp, sob, or howl.

Ring of coffee stain
on his breakfast napkin.

Brown, his eyes tinged
with smoke and gin.

The slap of his hand
against my ginger-brown skin.

The way I dragged my feet
to school.

The frown that encircled me
as I peered at his

brown casket. These days
I grind brown—like figs.

THE WRIGHT ORIGINS

Red clay gleamed across your blunt face.
Chicago wind came, tucked it under leaves.
Your fingers cramped, itched every pen stroke.
Your muse clamped down on your brain.
Bigger belched out, busted your pen's shaft.
Your palms scanned, trawled Himes's quick words.
In Paris, French words doused your tongue.

DEPOSITION

What you mean, *it's all over boy?*
You nothin' but a slinkin' lizard man.
You trottin' 'round, 'spectin me to growl.
I see you, with your gizzard eyes.
You spoutin' cab loads of what ifs.
What you know 'bout them, Bessie, Mary?
You prowlin' and howlin', a jackal man.

THIS IS THE NEWS

Mista Wright, I say you done good.
When white lawmen muffled Negroes, it daunted
Blacks, tellin' whites they were slashed slates.
You were a bullet and a hammer,
Shootin' away lies, nailin' down the truth.
White folks turned away from your glare.
You branded the page colored, saddle brown.

EMMETT TILL BEFORE HIS ECLIPSE

Mississippi, flint-edged state
Where black folks' sweat kinked cotton,
Bored you, "Bobo," trickster boy.
You, a child of Chicago,
Precise with your mother's dimes
Swift hands laid linoleum
Lush, in white shirt, western tie.

WHEN I CONSIDER

the bloated mass that was his body,
tears stream from my hands,
my hands claw the ground
as if I could bring up the box
that houses his flesh.

If they could, my fingers would poke
life into his nostrils.
Revived, he would regale me
with the tale of his ill-gotten fate,
how he clung to his accusers'
every word—such as it was—
their skewed language.

His ears flushed as they shunted him off,
away from his uncle's cabin in the haze
of early morning to the place
where they laughed and danced
and cracked open their bottles of beer.

He told me how he flinched,
how his right eye twitched as they beat
him, how he snorted
as the .45 calibre grazed his temple.
Alas, though, he could not know the rest,
how his body descended into water,
water nebulous at first.

But then its blackness grew,
pouring over his mute, mucked face,
his right eye dangling from its socket.
At that moment, the river knew
his mama would read about him
in newspapers for weeks to come.

I imagine how all that water swallowed him
as though he were nothing more than flotsam.
If Emmett could have seen himself,
seen his body settle in the water,
he probably would have stopped to pray
that no one would remember him this way,
mangled oracle that he was.

TO A WHITE MAN WHO STILL REFUSES TO RECOGNIZE
HUEY NEWTON

Years ago, I wore a red blouse, green pants,
And a black tam.
And my fist was a wee bit bigger than a tangerine.

I was ready to fracture your grin with my eyes.
Puncture your lips until they shriveled up like burnt peas.
Feel your eyes snap under my gaze like chicken bones.

I wanted to make your brain do a handspring,
Then cut it up thin,
Until it looked like slices of salami.

Then I wanted you to roast,
Until your body's smoke reminded you of my face.
You.You.You. I.I.I.

Wanted you to call my name.
Spray it all over your walls
Until its graffito rattled in your head.

Perhaps you would refuse to hold me.
Your bottle filled with my ink would explode,
The shards of you scattering along the street.

And no, you couldn't rinse me
Out of your blood,
Though you wanted to. You couldn't.

FATHER'S FAVORITE THINGS AND PEOPLE

Charlie Mingus' albums
social tea biscuits
brown wool coat
The Yankees
Valencia oranges
books by Chester Himes
Brut After Shave Lotion
Cadillac Coupe de Ville
striped shirts
Harlem's Better Crust Pie Bakery
New York Giants
Duke Ellington
muenster cheese
James Van Der Zee's photographs
books by John Hope Franklin
carrot cake
Louis Armstrong
English Leather Cologne
cow tongue
Brooks Brothers gray and blue suits
sweet potato pie
cowboy jeans
Billie Holiday
collard greens
Jackie Robinson
black-eyed peas
New York Jets green cap
hog's head cheese

Note

Hog's head cheese is seasoned meat made from parts of the head and feet of a hog.

DEEPER THAN SKIN

Negro blood is sure powerful because just one drop of black blood
makes a colored man.

—Langston Hughes

Negro—word I sipped and steeped in my
blood one quarter of a century. African American
is smoother, like whip cream on the tongue,
sure as red digits on a radio clock,
powerful—water spurting from a showerhead
because African American fits like an ao dai,
just shimmers against my bones, admonishes
one to displace words that sour breath. I
drop lies like scraps and horde suitcases
of facts for my nieces and nephews. What
black slave hands planted simmers in the
blood of a man whose hand grasps babies,
makes babies fly out of wombs with forceps,
a hand that snips umbilical cords of babies,
colored or white. Ellison wrote of an invisible
man. I write the world colorless as ether.

A former two-year college English instructor, Poet/Performer Grace C. Ocasio lives in Charlotte, North Carolina, with her husband, Edwin, and her daughter, Chloe. Twice a finalist for the Rash Award in Poetry (2010, 2013), Grace C. Ocasio is a recipient of the 2014 North Carolina Arts Council-funded Regional Artist Project Grant Award. She won honorable mention in the 2012 James Applewhite Poetry Prize competition. She won the Sonia Sanchez and Amiri Baraka Prize in Poetry in 2011 and was a scholarship recipient to the 2011 Napa Valley Writers' Conference. She also won second prize in the James Larkin Pearson free verse category of an annual poetry contest sponsored by the Poetry Council of North Carolina in 2008. Her poetry has appeared in *Rattle*, *Earth's Daughters*, *Haight Ashbury Literary Journal*, *Court Green*, p*hati'tude Literary Magazine*, *Obsidian*, *Blast Furnace Press*, *The Broad River Review*, the *North Carolina Literary Review*, and other journals. Her chapbook, *Hollerin from This Shack*, was published by Ahadada Books in 2009. She has also published essays in other publications including *The Charlotte Observer* and *InterRace*. She is a Soul Mountain Retreat fellow and Frost Place alumna. She also served as a reviewer for the online writers' resource, *The Review Review* in 2008 and 2009. Currently, she serves as a contributing editor for *Backbone Poetry Journal*. She is a member of the Association of Writing and Writing Programs, the Carolina African American Writers' Collective, the North Carolina Poetry Society, the North Carolina Writers' Network, and the Charlotte Writers' Club. She has read at venues that include the Harvey B. Gantt Center for African-American Arts and Culture in Charlotte, North Carolina; North Carolina A&T State University in Greensboro, North Carolina; the Florence Griswold Museum in Old Lyme, Connecticut; the East Bay Meeting House in Charleston, South Carolina; UNC Chapel Hill's Bull's Head Bookshop in Chapel Hill, North Carolina; and the Sensoria Festival at Central Piedmont Community College in Charlotte, North Carolina. She received her MFA in Poetry from Sarah Lawrence College, her MA in English from the University of North Carolina at Charlotte, and her BA in Print Journalism and English from Howard University, graduating *cum laude*.

Made in the USA
Monee, IL
07 July 2026

56551606R00062